Pregi Journal

This Book
Belongs To

....

....

....

First Exciting Experiences When?

Positive Pregnancy Test _____

Ultra Sound _____

Food Cravings _____

Felt Baby Kick _____

Hiccups _____

Felt Contraction _____

Heard Heartbeat _____

Other Memorable First exciting _____

First Ultrasound

Date	Weight	Length	Note

Our Reaction Moment

Our Family Reaction Moment

Appointment

Date	Time	Address	Purpose

Notes : _____

_____

_____

_____

_____

Appointment

Date	Time	Address	Purpose

Notes : _____

_____

_____

_____

_____

Appointment

Date	Time	Address	Purpose

Notes : _____

_____

_____

_____

_____

_____

Medication

Medication	Date	Time	Taken
			☐
			☐
			☐
			☐
			☐
			☐
			☐
			☐
			☐
			☐
			☐
			☐
			☐
			☐
			☐
			☐

Medication

Medication	Date	Time	Taken
			⬜
			⬜
			⬜
			⬜
			⬜
			⬜
			⬜
			⬜
			⬜
			⬜
			⬜
			⬜
			⬜
			⬜
			⬜
			⬜

Medication

Medication	Date	Time	Taken
			☐
			☐
			☐
			☐
			☐
			☐
			☐
			☐
			☐
			☐
			☐
			☐
			☐
			☐
			☐
			☐

Medication

Medication	Date	Time	Taken
			▪
			▪
			▪
			▪
			▪
			▪
			▪
			▪
			▪
			▪
			▪
			▪
			▪
			▪
			▪
			▪

Medication

Medication	Date	Time	Taken
			☐
			☐
			☐
			☐
			☐
			☐
			☐
			☐
			☐
			☐
			☐
			☐
			☐
			☐
			☐
			☐
			☐

Hospital Packing List

For Mama	For Baby

Hospital Packing List

For Mama	For Baby

Hospital Packing List

For Mama	For Baby

Who I Want In The Delivery Room

Type Of Birth

- Vaginal
- Water Birth
- C-Section
- VBAC

Who Is Most Important To Me

Baby Shower Invitation

Date

Time

Location

Throughn by

Favorite Gift

Favorite Moment

Baby Shower Invitation Guest List

Name	Phone	Address

Baby Shower Invitation Guest List

Name	Phone	Address

Week _____   Date _____

Belly Size _____   Weight _____

Health

| |
| |

Emotional Health

| |
| |

Food That Calms My Belly

| |
| |

Food That Upset My Belly

| |
| |

I'm Craving

| |
| |

Symptoms

| |
| |

Moment to Remember

| |
| |

Notes

| |
| |

Week _____   Date _____

Belly Size _____   Weight _____

Health

Emotional Health

Food That Calms My Belly

Food That Upset My Belly

I'm Craving

Symptoms

Moment to Remember

Notes

Week _____   Date _____

Belly Size _____   Weight _____

Health

Emotional Health

Food That Calms My Belly

Food That Upset My Belly

I'm Craving

Symptoms

Moment to Remember

Notes

Week _____   Date _____

Belly Size _____   Weight _____

Health

Emotional Health

Food That Calms My Belly

Food That Upset My Belly

I'm Craving

Symptoms

Moment to Remember

Notes

Week _____   Date _____

Belly Size _____   Weight _____

Health

Emotional Health

Food That Calms My Belly

Food That Upset My Belly

I'm Craving

Symptoms

Moment to Remember

Notes

Week _____   Date _____

Belly Size _____   Weight _____

Health

Emotional Health

Food That Calms My Belly

Food That Upset My Belly

I'm Craving

Symptoms

Moment to Remember

Notes

Week _____

Date _____

Belly Size _____

Weight _____

Health

[blank box]

Emotional Health

[blank box]

Food That Calms My Belly

[blank box]

Food That Upset My Belly

[blank box]

I'm Craving

[blank box]

Symptoms

[blank box]

Moment to Remember

[blank box]

Notes

[blank box]

Week _____

Date _____

Belly Size _____

Weight _____

Health

Emotional Health

Food That Calms My Belly

Food That Upset My Belly

I'm Craving

Symptoms

Moment to Remember

Notes

Week _____   Date _____

Belly Size _____   Weight _____

Health

Emotional Health

Food That Calms My Belly

Food That Upset My Belly

I'm Craving

Symptoms

Moment to Remember

Notes

Week _____   Date _____

Belly Size _____   Weight _____

Health

Emotional Health

Food That Calms My Belly

Food That Upset My Belly

I'm Craving

Symptoms

Moment to Remember

Notes

Week _____   Date _____

Belly Size _____   Weight _____

Health

Emotional Health

Food That Calms My Belly

Food That Upset My Belly

I'm Craving

Symptoms

Moment to Remember

Notes

Week _____   Date _____

Belly Size _____   Weight _____

Health

Emotional Health

Food That Calms My Belly

Food That Upset My Belly

I'm Craving

Symptoms

Moment to Remember

Notes

Week _____   Date _____

Belly Size _____   Weight _____

Health

Emotional Health

Food That Calms My Belly

Food That Upset My Belly

I'm Craving

Symptoms

Moment to Remember

Notes

Week _____   Date _____

Belly Size _____   Weight _____

Health

Emotional Health

Food That Calms My Belly

Food That Upset My Belly

I'm Craving

Symptoms

Moment to Remember

Notes

Week _____   Date _____

Belly Size _____   Weight _____

Health

Emotional Health

Food That Calms My Belly

Food That Upset My Belly

I'm Craving

Symptoms

Moment to Remember

Notes

Week _____   Date _____

Belly Size _____   Weight _____

Health

Emotional Health

Food That Calms My Belly

Food That Upset My Belly

I'm Craving

Symptoms

Moment to Remember

Notes

Week _____   Date _____

Belly Size _____   Weight _____

Health

[ ]

Emotional Health

[ ]

Food That Calms My Belly

[ ]

Food That Upset My Belly

[ ]

I'm Craving

[ ]

Symptoms

[ ]

Moment to Remember

[ ]

Notes

[ ]

Week _____   Date _____

Belly Size _____   Weight _____

Health

Emotional Health

Food That Calms My Belly

Food That Upset My Belly

I'm Craving

Symptoms

Moment to Remember

Notes

Week _____   Date _____

Belly Size _____   Weight _____

Health

Emotional Health

Food That Calms My Belly

Food That Upset My Belly

I'm Craving

Symptoms

Moment to Remember

Notes

Week _____   Date _____

Belly Size _____   Weight _____

Health

Emotional Health

Food That Calms My Belly

Food That Upset My Belly

I'm Craving

Symptoms

Moment to Remember

Notes

Week _____   Date _____

Belly Size _____   Weight _____

Health

Emotional Health

Food That Calms My Belly

Food That Upset My Belly

I'm Craving

Symptoms

Moment to Remember

Notes

Week _____   Date _____

Belly Size _____   Weight _____

Health

Emotional Health

Food That Calms My Belly

Food That Upset My Belly

I'm Craving

Symptoms

Moment to Remember

Notes

Week _____   Date _____

Belly Size _____   Weight _____

Health

Emotional Health

Food That Calms My Belly

Food That Upset My Belly

I'm Craving

Symptoms

Moment to Remember

Notes

Week _____   Date _____

Belly Size _____   Weight _____

Health

Emotional Health

Food That Calms My Belly

Food That Upset My Belly

I'm Craving

Symptoms

Moment to Remember

Notes

Week _____   Date _____

Belly Size _____   Weight _____

Health

Emotional Health

Food That Calms My Belly

Food That Upset My Belly

I'm Craving

Symptoms

Moment to Remember

Notes

Week _____   Date _____

Belly Size _____   Weight _____

Health

Emotional Health

Food That Calms My Belly

Food That Upset My Belly

I'm Craving

Symptoms

Moment to Remember

Notes

Week _____   **Date** _____

Belly Size _____   **Weight** _____

Health

Emotional Health

Food That Calms My Belly

Food That Upset My Belly

I'm Craving

Symptoms

Moment to Remember

Notes

Week _____   Date _____

Belly Size _____   Weight _____

Health

Emotional Health

Food That Calms My Belly

Food That Upset My Belly

I'm Craving

Symptoms

Moment to Remember

Notes

Week _____   **Date** _____

Belly Size _____   **Weight** _____

Health

Emotional Health

Food That Calms My Belly

Food That Upset My Belly

I'm Craving

Symptoms

Moment to Remember

Notes

Week _____   Date _____

Belly Size _____   Weight _____

Health

Emotional Health

Food That Calms My Belly

Food That Upset My Belly

I'm Craving

Symptoms

Moment to Remember

Notes

Week _____   Date _____

Belly Size _____   Weight _____

Health

Emotional Health

Food That Calms My Belly

Food That Upset My Belly

I'm Craving

Symptoms

Moment to Remember

Notes

Week _____   Date _____

Belly Size _____   Weight _____

Health

Emotional Health

Food That Calms My Belly

Food That Upset My Belly

I'm Craving

Symptoms

Moment to Remember

Notes

Week _____   Date _____

Belly Size _____   ## Weight _____

Health

Emotional Health

Food That Calms My Belly

Food That Upset My Belly

I'm Craving

Symptoms

Moment to Remember

Notes

Week _____   Date _____

Belly Size _____   Weight _____

Health

Emotional Health

Food That Calms My Belly

Food That Upset My Belly

I'm Craving

Symptoms

Moment to Remember

Notes

Week _____　　**Date** _____

Belly Size _____　　**Weight** _____

Health

Emotional Health

Food That Calms My Belly

Food That Upset My Belly

I'm Craving

Symptoms

Moment to Remember

Notes

Week _____

Date _____

Belly Size _____

Weight _____

Health

Emotional Health

Food That Calms My Belly

Food That Upset My Belly

I'm Craving

Symptoms

Moment to Remember

Notes

Week _____   Date _____

Belly Size _____   Weight _____

Health

Emotional Health

Food That Calms My Belly

Food That Upset My Belly

I'm Craving

Symptoms

Moment to Remember

Notes

Week _____   Date _____

Belly Size _____   Weight _____

Health

Emotional Health

Food That Calms My Belly

Food That Upset My Belly

I'm Craving

Symptoms

Moment to Remember

Notes

Week _____   Date _____

Belly Size _____   Weight _____

Health

Emotional Health

Food That Calms My Belly

Food That Upset My Belly

I'm Craving

Symptoms

Moment to Remember

Notes

Week _____   Date _____

Belly Size _____   Weight _____

Health

Emotional Health

Food That Calms My Belly

Food That Upset My Belly

I'm Craving

Symptoms

Moment to Remember

Notes

Week _____

Date _____

Belly Size _____

Weight _____

Health

Emotional Health

Food That Calms My Belly

Food That Upset My Belly

I'm Craving

Symptoms

Moment to Remember

Notes

Week _____   Date _____

Belly Size _____   Weight _____

Health

[ ]

Emotional Health

[ ]

Food That Calms My Belly

[ ]

Food That Upset My Belly

[ ]

I'm Craving

[ ]

Symptoms

[ ]

Moment to Remember

[ ]

Notes

[ ]

Week _____ **Date** _____

Belly Size _____ **Weight** _____

Health

Emotional Health

Food That Calms My Belly

Food That Upset My Belly

I'm Craving

Symptoms

Moment to Remember

Notes

Week _____   Date _____

Belly Size _____   Weight _____

Health

Emotional Health

Food That Calms My Belly

Food That Upset My Belly

I'm Craving

Symptoms

Moment to Remember

Notes

Week _____   Date _____

Belly Size _____   Weight _____

Health

Emotional Health

Food That Calms My Belly

Food That Upset My Belly

I'm Craving

Symptoms

Moment to Remember

Notes

Week _____   Date _____

Belly Size _____   Weight _____

Health

Emotional Health

Food That Calms My Belly

Food That Upset My Belly

I'm Craving

Symptoms

Moment to Remember

Notes

Week _____   Date _____

Belly Size _____   Weight _____

Health

Emotional Health

Food That Calms My Belly

Food That Upset My Belly

I'm Craving

Symptoms

Moment to Remember

Notes

Week _____   Date _____

Belly Size _____   Weight _____

Health

Emotional Health

Food That Calms My Belly

Food That Upset My Belly

I'm Craving

Symptoms

Moment to Remember

Notes

Week _____

Date _____

Belly Size _____

Weight _____

Health

Emotional Health

Food That Calms My Belly

Food That Upset My Belly

I'm Craving

Symptoms

Moment to Remember

Notes

Week _____   Date _____

Belly Size _____   Weight _____

Health

Emotional Health

Food That Calms My Belly

Food That Upset My Belly

I'm Craving

Symptoms

Moment to Remember

Notes

Week _____   **Date** _____

Belly Size _____   **Weight** _____

Health

Emotional Health

Food That Calms My Belly

Food That Upset My Belly

I'm Craving

Symptoms

Moment to Remember

Notes

Week _____   Date _____

Belly Size _____   Weight _____

Health

Emotional Health

Food That Calms My Belly

Food That Upset My Belly

I'm Craving

Symptoms

Moment to Remember

Notes

Week _____   Date _____

Belly Size _____   Weight _____

Health

[ ]

Emotional Health

[ ]

Food That Calms My Belly

[ ]

Food That Upset My Belly

[ ]

I'm Craving

[ ]

Symptoms

[ ]

Moment to Remember

[ ]

Notes

[ ]

Week _____

Date _____

Belly Size _____

Weight _____

Health

Emotional Health

Food That Calms My Belly

Food That Upset My Belly

I'm Craving

Symptoms

Moment to Remember

Notes

Week _____

Date _____

Belly Size _____

Weight _____

Health

Emotional Health

Food That Calms My Belly

Food That Upset My Belly

I'm Craving

Symptoms

Moment to Remember

Notes

Week _____   Date _____

Belly Size _____   Weight _____

Health

Emotional Health

Food That Calms My Belly

Food That Upset My Belly

I'm Craving

Symptoms

Moment to Remember

Notes

Week _____   **Date** _____

Belly Size _____   **Weight** _____

Health

Emotional Health

Food That Calms My Belly

Food That Upset My Belly

I'm Craving

Symptoms

Moment to Remember

Notes

Week _____   Date _____

Belly Size _____   Weight _____

Health

Emotional Health

Food That Calms My Belly

Food That Upset My Belly

I'm Craving

Symptoms

Moment to Remember

Notes

Week _____

Date _____

Belly Size _____

Weight _____

Health

Emotional Health

Food That Calms My Belly

Food That Upset My Belly

I'm Craving

Symptoms

Moment to Remember

Notes

Week _____   Date _____

Belly Size _____   Weight _____

Health

I'm Craving

Food That Calms My Belly   Food That Upset My Belly

Emotional Health

Symptoms   Moment to Remember

Notes

Week _____   Date _____

Belly Size _____   Weight _____

Health

Emotional Health

Food That Calms My Belly

Food That Upset My Belly

I'm Craving

Symptoms

Moment to Remember

Notes

Week _____   Date _____

Belly Size _____   Weight _____

Health

Emotional Health

Food That Calms My Belly

Food That Upset My Belly

I'm Craving

Symptoms

Moment to Remember

Notes

Week _____   Date _____

Belly Size _____ Weight _____

Health

Emotional Health

Food That Calms My Belly

Food That Upset My Belly

I'm Craving

Symptoms

Moment to Remember

Notes

Week _____   Date _____

Belly Size _____   Weight _____

Health

Emotional Health

Food That Calms My Belly

Food That Upset My Belly

I'm Craving

Symptoms

Moment to Remember

Notes

Week _____   Date _____

Belly Size _____   Weight _____

Health

Emotional Health

Food That Calms My Belly

Food That Upset My Belly

I'm Craving

Symptoms

Moment to Remember

Notes

Week _____

Date _____

Belly Size _____

Weight _____

Health

Emotional Health

Food That Calms My Belly

Food That Upset My Belly

I'm Craving

Symptoms

Moment to Remember

Notes

Week _____   Date _____

Belly Size _____   Weight _____

Health

Emotional Health

Food That Calms My Belly

Food That Upset My Belly

I'm Craving

Symptoms

Moment to Remember

Notes

Week _____   Date _____

Belly Size _____   Weight _____

Health

Emotional Health

Food That Calms My Belly

Food That Upset My Belly

I'm Craving

Symptoms

Moment to Remember

Notes

Week _____   Date _____

Belly Size _____   Weight _____

Health

Emotional Health

Food That Calms My Belly

Food That Upset My Belly

I'm Craving

Symptoms

Moment to Remember

Notes

Week _____   Date _____

Belly Size _____   Weight _____

Health

Emotional Health

Food That Calms My Belly

Food That Upset My Belly

I'm Craving

Symptoms

Moment to Remember

Notes

Week _____   Date _____

Belly Size _____   Weight _____

Health

Emotional Health

Food That Calms My Belly

Food That Upset My Belly

I'm Craving

Symptoms

Moment to Remember

Notes

Week _____   Date _____

Belly Size _____   Weight _____

Health

Emotional Health

Food That Calms My Belly

Food That Upset My Belly

I'm Craving

Symptoms

Moment to Remember

Notes

Week _____

Date _____

Belly Size _____

Weight _____

Health

Emotional Health

Food That Calms My Belly

Food That Upset My Belly

I'm Craving

Symptoms

Moment to Remember

Notes

Week _____   Date _____

Belly Size _____   Weight _____

Health

Emotional Health

Food That Calms My Belly

Food That Upset My Belly

I'm Craving

Symptoms

Moment to Remember

Notes

Week _____   **Date** _____

Belly Size _____   **Weight** _____

Health

Emotional Health

Food That Calms My Belly

Food That Upset My Belly

I'm Craving

Symptoms

Moment to Remember

Notes

Week _____

Date _____

Belly Size _____

Weight _____

Health

Emotional Health

Food That Calms My Belly

Food That Upset My Belly

I'm Craving

Symptoms

Moment to Remember

Notes

Week _____   Date _____

Belly Size _____   Weight _____

Health

Emotional Health

Food That Calms My Belly

Food That Upset My Belly

I'm Craving

Symptoms

Moment to Remember

Notes

Week _____   Date _____

Belly Size _____   Weight _____

Health

Emotional Health

Food That Calms My Belly

Food That Upset My Belly

I'm Craving

Symptoms

Moment to Remember

Notes

Week _____   **Date** _____

Belly Size _____   **Weight** _____

Health

Emotional Health

Food That Calms My Belly

Food That Upset My Belly

I'm Craving

Symptoms

Moment to Remember

Notes

Week _____   Date _____

Belly Size _____   Weight _____

Health

Emotional Health

Food That Calms My Belly

Food That Upset My Belly

I'm Craving

Symptoms

Moment to Remember

Notes

Week _____

Date _____

Belly Size _____

Weight _____

Health

Emotional Health

Food That Calms My Belly

Food That Upset My Belly

I'm Craving

Symptoms

Moment to Remember

Notes

Week _____   Date _____

Belly Size _____   Weight _____

Health

[ ]

Emotional Health

[ ]

Food That Calms My Belly

[ ]

Food That Upset My Belly

[ ]

I'm Craving

[ ]

Symptoms

[ ]

Moment to Remember

[ ]

Notes

[ ]

Week _____   **Date** _____

Belly Size _____   **Weight** _____

Health

Emotional Health

Food That Calms My Belly

Food That Upset My Belly

I'm Craving

Symptoms

Moment to Remember

Notes

Week _____   Date _____

Belly Size _____   Weight _____

Health

Emotional Health

Food That Calms My Belly

Food That Upset My Belly

I'm Craving

Symptoms

Moment to Remember

Notes

Week _____   Date _____

Belly Size _____   Weight _____

Health

```

```

Emotional Health

```

```

Food That Calms My Belly

```

```

Food That Upset My Belly

```

```

I'm Craving

```

```

Symptoms

```

```

Moment to Remember

```

```

Notes

```

```

Week _____   Date _____

Belly Size _____   Weight _____

Health

Emotional Health

Food That Calms My Belly

Food That Upset My Belly

I'm Craving

Symptoms

Moment to Remember

Notes

Week _____   Date _____

Belly Size _____   Weight _____

Health

Emotional Health

Food That Calms My Belly

Food That Upset My Belly

I'm Craving

Symptoms

Moment to Remember

Notes

Week _____   Date _____

Belly Size _____   Weight _____

Health

Emotional Health

Food That Calms My Belly

Food That Upset My Belly

I'm Craving

Symptoms

Moment to Remember

Notes

Week _____   Date _____

Belly Size _____   Weight _____

Health

Emotional Health

Food That Calms My Belly

Food That Upset My Belly

I'm Craving

Symptoms

Moment to Remember

Notes

Week _____   Date _____

Belly Size _____   Weight _____

Health

Emotional Health

Food That Calms My Belly

Food That Upset My Belly

I'm Craving

Symptoms

Moment to Remember

Notes

Week _____   Date _____

Belly Size _____   Weight _____

Health

Emotional Health

Food That Calms My Belly

Food That Upset My Belly

I'm Craving

Symptoms

Moment to Remember

Notes

Week _____   Date _____

Belly Size _____   Weight _____

Health

Emotional Health

Food That Calms My Belly

Food That Upset My Belly

I'm Craving

Symptoms

Moment to Remember

Notes

Week _____   Date _____

Belly Size _____   Weight _____

Health

Emotional Health

Food That Calms My Belly

Food That Upset My Belly

I'm Craving

Symptoms

Moment to Remember

Notes

Week _____

Date _____

Belly Size _____

Weight _____

Health

Emotional Health

Food That Calms My Belly

Food That Upset My Belly

I'm Craving

Symptoms

Moment to Remember

Notes

Week _____

Date _____

Belly Size _____

Weight _____

Health

Emotional Health

Food That Calms My Belly

Food That Upset My Belly

I'm Craving

Symptoms

Moment to Remember

Notes

Week _____   Date _____

Belly Size _____   Weight _____

Health

Emotional Health

Food That Calms My Belly

Food That Upset My Belly

I'm Craving

Symptoms

Moment to Remember

Notes

Week _____   Date _____

Belly Size _____   Weight _____

Health

Emotional Health

Food That Calms My Belly

Food That Upset My Belly

I'm Craving

Symptoms

Moment to Remember

Notes

Week _____   Date _____

Belly Size _____   Weight _____

Health

Emotional Health

Food That Calms My Belly

Food That Upset My Belly

I'm Craving

Symptoms

Moment to Remember

Notes

Week _____

Date _____

Belly Size _____

Weight _____

Health

Emotional Health

Food That Calms My Belly

Food That Upset My Belly

I'm Craving

Symptoms

Moment to Remember

Notes

Notes

Date _____

Notes

Notes

Date _____

Notes

Date _____

Printed in Great Britain
by Amazon

24652961R00071